DRUG
DANGERS

TRANQUILIZER, BARBITURATE, AND DOWNER
DRUG DANGERS

Michelle M. Houle

Enslow Publishers, Inc.

40 Industrial Road ～   PO Box 38
Box 398   Aldershot
Berkeley Heights, NJ 07922   Hants GU12 6BP
USA   UK

http://www.enslow.com

Library of Congress Cataloging-in-Publication Data

Houle, Michelle M.
   Tranquilizer, barbiturate, and downer drug dangers / Michelle M. Houle.
      p.   cm. — (Drug dangers)
   Includes bibliographical references and index.
   Summary: Describes the effects of drug abuse on body and mind as
well as on the larger society and indicates ways to prevent and fight
destructive drug habits.
   ISBN 0-7660-1320-0
   1. Drug abuse Juvenile literature. 2. Narcotic habit Juvenile
literature. 3. Tranquilizing drugs Juvenile literature. 4. Barbiturates
Juvenile literature. [1. Drug abuse. 2. Narcotic habit. 3. Tranquilizing
drugs. 4. Barbiturates.]
   I. Title II. Series.
   RC564.3.H68   2000
   362.29—dc21   99-20150
                                                           CIP

Printed in the United States of America

10 9 8 7 6 5 4 3 2 1

Every effort has been made to locate all copyright holders of material used in
this book. If any errors or omissions have occurred, corrections will be made in
future editions of this book.

To Our Readers:
All Internet addresses in this book were active and appropriate when we
went to press. Any comments or suggestions can be sent by e-mail to
Comments@enslow.com or to the address on the back cover.

Photo Credits: © Copyright 1997, 1996 T/Maker Company, p. 35; Corel
Corporation, pp. 13, 18, 21, 45; Diamar Interactive Corp., pp. 47, 52; ©
Digital Stock, p. 19; © George Rekela, p. 24; National Archives, pp. 31, 32, 39,
40; Photofest, pp. 6, 26, 27.

Cover Photo: © Thierry Cariou/The Stock Market

contents

Titles in the **Drug Dangers** series:

one

A Rainbow's End

The most memorable song from *The Wizard of Oz*, "Over the Rainbow," takes on a whole new meaning when you look at the life of the actress who played the main character, Dorothy. At the age of sixteen, Judy Garland changed the course of movie history with her performance as the Kansas girl who is swept away to a dreamland with her dog, Toto. Garland rocketed to stardom with the film in 1939, but her life began to slowly spiral downward at the same time because of her drug use.

Judy Garland was born in 1922 and began working for MGM Studios as an actress when she was only thirteen. At that time, the children involved in the film industry were constantly working, and when they were not filming, they went to school whenever they could. Judy was becoming very popular with movie-watching

Judy Garland was only sixteen when she played the role of Dorothy in *The Wizard of Oz*. The demanding film role and hectic schedules, however, began to wear her down. Doctors first gave her amphetamines, or "uppers," for energy, and later gave her barbiturates to calm her.

audiences, and she was in demand by the studio. Unfortunately, the hectic schedule of the studio began to wear her down.

To help Garland, the studio doctors gave her some pills. At the time, no one knew that the pills could be addictive or harmful and no one worried about young people using them. The pills seemed like "marvelous elixirs [magic cures]."[1] Judy, like many other young actors and actresses of the time, took amphetamines, or "uppers," to give her energy for filming and to keep her weight down. However, she was so high on amphetamines that she could not sleep at night. Thinking they were helping the young star, doctors gave her barbiturates to sedate her into sleep. The constant up and down would take its toll on her personal and professional life.

Later in her life, Judy Garland told people that her

troubles with drugs began when she was about fourteen. She even thought the studio might have tried to hide drugs in her food so that she would not know how much she was taking.[2] Eventually, she could not get through a day without these drugs, which she later called her "medicine." There would be times in her life when she realized how serious her addictions were, but her need for the drugs was something that began when she was so young that it was difficult for her to break the habit. It was a habit that would eventually kill her.

Judy Garland's life was full of mental and physical ups and downs. She was married five times and had three children—Liza Minnelli, and Lorna and Joe Luft. All the while, she was starring in films and on stage—and at the same time building a reputation as an unpredictable performer, generally as a result of her frequent drug use. Sometimes she would show up late for a rehearsal or for filming because she had taken so many barbiturates that she could not wake up in the morning. Sometimes she would not even show up at all. Once, she overdosed on sleeping pills on the day of a big television special. Her husband at the time, Sid Luft, tried to wake her up, but she was very sluggish. Through the beginning part of the show, even the audience could tell that there was something wrong—it was as if she was moving in slow motion.

Despite all of this, Judy Garland remained a symbol of a fantasy life to her fans. Perhaps they saw her as Dorothy, not the actress who played her. Perhaps they did not want to realize that their idol was a serious drug addict whose actions were hurting her, her children, and other people she loved. Judy Garland suffered multiple drug overdoses that sent her to the hospital many times. The drugs caused horrible mood swings, and she attempted suicide more than once. Overall, the drugs made her incapable of behaving normally, even with her family.

More than thirty years of drug use came to an end when Judy Garland died of an overdose of Seconal™, a barbiturate. She was forty-seven years old. People think that she took the pills to help her sleep and that she mistakenly took too many. Her death was ruled accidental—there were no signs of suicide. Judy Garland had finally lost the serious battle against downer drugs.

two

Social Effects of Downer Drugs

"If anxiety is an inevitable part of the human condition, then the wish for a magic potion to banish anxiety is probably a timeless human desire."[1]

Imagine you have a big test tomorrow. It is the biggest test of the year, and you have studied very hard. This test could determine your entire grade, and you would like to do well. You probably feel nervous—it would be natural to feel that way.

Now think about what you would do if you felt nervous all the time. It is one thing to be a little worried before a test or a big game, but some people feel this way every day, no matter what is happening in their lives. Some people feel too nervous and stressed in situations that should not cause such worries. For example, they may feel overly nervous and worried about going to the grocery store or about simply going into their school, even if there are no tests planned for the day.

This nervous feeling is also known as *anxiety*, a word that describes what happens when people worry about things that could hurt their feelings—not their bodies—regardless of whether or not those things have happened yet.[2] Some people have such strong anxiety that they cannot think about anything else. The anxiety may take over their lives, making it difficult to work, sleep, or even enjoy themselves with friends or family. These people may not be able to handle everyday situations. Hopefully, they will go to their doctor to ask for help.

At the doctor's office, overly anxious people might be told that they should go to counseling to help control this nervousness or that a change in lifestyle might be helpful. Sometimes, however, doctors decide that people need something more to help them. If this is the case, a doctor might prescribe some sort of medication to help someone calm down and live life more normally. These prescription drugs have many different names, but as a group, they are called sedative-hypnotics, or tranquilizers, and some people informally refer to them as downers. These drugs affect the central nervous system, the system of nerves and nerve cells that controls the body's physical and behavioral reactions. Because they slow down, or depress, the actions of the central nervous system, these drugs are also called depressants. Used in small amounts, sedative medications may help a person relax, but in large doses, they can put someone to sleep.[3]

Physical Effects of Downer Drugs

A sedative or tranquilizer helps a person feel tranquil or calm. These drugs can have some of the following effects:

Possible Positive Effects of Downer Drugs

- Lowered inhibitions or fears

- Muscle relaxation

- Sedation, or calming

- Hypnosis, or sleep

- General anesthesia (the loss of pain to part or all of the body)

Because these drugs make people calm, someone who is overly anxious might have an easier time with everyday activities after taking a sedative or tranquilizer.

Aside from easing anxiety, however, these drugs have many other benefits. For example, people who have insomnia, or difficulty sleeping, would welcome the effects of this medication because it would help them overcome that problem and get some sleep. A tranquilizing drug such as Valium™ can also help stop seizures when given by intravenous injection, an injection of the medicine directly into a vein. Valium reduces the risk of seizures in people who are prone to them.[4] Downer drugs can also be used as painkillers. This makes them helpful during surgery and useful for people who have constant and severe pain due to an accident or disease.

People might think that these are "miracle drugs" because they do so many helpful things. It is important, however, to recognize that no drug is perfect, or even positive, in every way. Negative things can happen even when a person is using a drug as the doctor ordered. These negative effects are often known as side effects. For example, users of tranquilizers must be careful driving a car because these medications can cause drowsiness. Falling asleep at the wheel could be a deadly consequence.

Possible Negative Effects of Downer Drugs

- Lowered inhibitions or fears

- Slurred speech or slow and clumsy body movements

- Confusion

- Dizziness

- Poor memory and/or confused judgment

- Short attention span

- Sedation, or calming

- Hypnosis, or sleep

- General anesthesia (the loss of pain to part or all of the body)

- Coma/shock

- Death

Users of tranquilizers must be careful if they drive when they are taking them, because tranquilizers can cause drowsiness. Falling asleep at the wheel could be a deadly consequence.

How tranquilizers affect users depends, to a degree, on the situation and conditions in which they are taken. Many people use downer drugs for legitimate medical problems, but some people use them for other reasons. But why would people use these drugs if they did not need to?

Why People Take Downer Drugs

Many people who are addicted to downer drugs first used them under a doctor's supervision. Perhaps they had been in an accident and were in pain, or perhaps they were going through a stressful time in their lives—someone close to them died or they lost a job. They may have taken the drugs to help with their anxiety. When these situations pass, however, some people find it difficult to stop their drug use. They also may have liked the way the drug made them feel. Though these medications are most often prescribed for short-term use, some people continue to use them for a very long time.

Inappropriate use of the drug does not make a tranquilizer or sedative a "bad drug." One doctor once said, "The only point that good and bad comes in is in the individual use of drugs."[5] A person might actually need the drug in order to soothe severe pain or to relieve intense anxiety. Therefore, the drug might be helpful and positive for some people. However, when people use drugs they do not need, or when they use them without a doctor's supervision, there is a serious problem. This is called drug abuse. With downer drugs, as with any other illegal drug, abuse can be very dangerous.

The *Los Angeles Times* describes prescription drug abuse as "Using more than prescribed more often than prescribed, for reasons other than prescribed, or without a prescription."[6] One doctor explained that some people use sedatives and tranquilizers not only for medical reasons but also may use them illegally. These people want to "induce euphoria, to drown out their emotional pain, or to try to feel normal by preventing withdrawal symptoms."[7]

Some people like the way the drugs make them feel, and they use the drugs to produce these feelings. *Euphoria* is a word often used to describe the high people feel when using sedatives and tranquilizers. Because the drug has a soothing effect, the user may feel happy and calm, which is *only* a result of the drug's ability to affect the mind. Drug users might not even notice the many real problems they face if they have taken too many downers.

Helpful or Harmful?

Drugs can be dangerous for a number of reasons. One of the most serious aspects of downer drugs is that they often cause dependence and tolerance. Dependence is what happens when a person takes a drug for an extended period and the body comes to expect and need the drug to function normally. Tolerance is what happens when the body needs more of a drug to cause the desired effects. Neither dependence nor tolerance is the same as abuse.

Drug abuse has been defined as "the continued use of a drug despite negative consequences." If a person continues to use a drug even if he or she does not need it medically and even if it is causing serious problems, he or she is probably an abuser.[8] A person is dependent on a drug if he or she experiences withdrawal symptoms. Withdrawal symptoms are the body's way of coping with the absence of the drug. The symptoms may include a return to anxiety or insomnia, but they may also be very serious and even life threatening. Withdrawal and overdose from tranquilizer use may be fatal. People must stop using downer drugs by slowly reducing the amount they take. An overdose occurs when the user takes more of a drug than the body can handle. Overdose with downer drugs can be particularly dangerous because these drugs may slow down all of the body's functions— even breathing. Many people die from downer drug overdoses unless they receive immediate medical help.

Which Drugs Are Which?

There are many different brand names of tranquilizers and sedative-hypnotics, and even these two titles can sometimes be used differently. Usually the word *tranquilizers* refers to drugs dispensed in a hospital for either the anesthesia or pain killing effects, and the word *sedatives* means sleeping pills. However, all these drugs can make a person tranquil, or calm. They all fall under the category of "depressants" or "downers" because they depress, or slow down, the central nervous system's actions. There are four major kinds of depressants (which will be explained in more detail in Chapter 4): the opiates and opioids, the sedative-hypnotics, alcohol, and solvents and inhalants. The chart below shows some, but not all, of the legal and illegal drugs that make up each category.

Many of the drugs on this chart can be very helpful to people. However, they are also often abused. Some of these are drugs that are often prescribed by doctors and that are often abused.

Prescription Drug Abuse
Although it might be surprising, it is possible to become dependent on a drug while under a doctor's supervision.

Types of Depressants

Opiates and Opioids	Sedative-hypnotics	Alcohol	Solvents and Inhalants
codeine heroin methadone morphine opium	barbiturates benzodiazepines	beer liquor wine	gasoline glue

Unfortunately, some people go beyond dependence and into abuse even if they are being watched by a doctor. Drug abusers will often go to great lengths to get their drugs, and they will often fool a lot of people along the way. Some patients "doctor-shop," meaning that they will go to more than one doctor to get more than one prescription at a time without any of the doctors or pharmacies figuring it out. Other people buy drugs from drug dealers who may have bought or stolen the drugs. The dealers could be selling prescription medication they got from doctors. Dealers may also have gotten the drugs from complete strangers—and, if this is the case, they may not know what is actually in the pills they are selling. People should always know exactly what drugs they are taking, and no one should ever take anyone else's prescription.

Many downer drugs change the way people act and interact with others. Depending on the circumstances, people on downer drugs might simply go to sleep or they might become upset and violent. Because of these different possibilities, downer drugs have been linked to many of today's social problems, such as crime and violence.

One of the most serious problems with these drugs is the fact that they cause people to act as if they are under the influence of alcohol. When people drink too much, they often behave very differently from the way they do when they are sober. Excessive drinking limits a person's ability to control his or her actions. One doctor said, "I often tell patients that the brain can't tell the difference between a shot of liquor and a Valium tablet."[9]

Downer drugs are known to make it difficult for a person to pay attention, and they seem to cause

Some people can become dependent on tranquilizers even while under a doctor's care. Some patients will go to several doctors and different pharmacies to get more than one prescription at a time without the individual doctors or pharmacies finding out.

problems with memory and coordination.[10] These side effects, in addition to the possibility of severe drowsiness, are the reason people should be concerned about driving a car and operating machinery while they are using depressants. One study even showed that people who took benzodiazepines, a specific kind of downer drug, make more trips to the doctor and are more likely to have to go to the emergency room because of an accident than people who do not take benzodiazepines.[11]

Another aspect of downer drug abuse and misuse that affects society is crime. Drug abusers often run out of money quickly because they spend so much to support their habit. In order to make money and buy more drugs, some abusers turn to prostitution, drug dealing, and burglary. In some situations, downer drug users may be very aggressive and even violent. When people's inhibitions are lowered, they are more likely to do things they would not normally do, and sometimes this comes at the cost of pain to themselves and to others. There is also a link between the use of depressants and suicide among young people.[12] Because downer drugs may also induce a depression of both body and mind, users may not realize the seriousness of what they are doing. And they may not realize that the drugs are causing them to be more upset and depressed than they would be otherwise.

Because downer drug users do not always realize the seriousness of their actions, they are at risk of contracting AIDS, hepatitis, and other diseases that are transmitted sexually or through the sharing of needles. For example, a drug-using person may engage in unprotected sex, one way in which the AIDS virus can be passed from person to person. It is also dangerous for people to share needles

Sometimes people who develop a dependence on tranquilizers may turn to a life of crime to find money to buy more drugs.

while using downer drugs. If the needle is not clean, a user might inject someone else's diseased blood into his or her own body—another way in which the AIDS virus is spread. Also, abusers may inject unknown substances into their blood since drugs bought on the street can contain anything from powdered milk to bathroom cleaners.[13]

The Date Rape Drug

One of the most dangerous tranquilizers is Rohypnol™, a benzodiazepine that has been called the "date-rape drug" because of the sexual assaults that have been linked to its use. The drug, pronounced "roe-HIP-nol," and sometimes called "roofies" or "roach," is made by the Swiss drug company Hoffman La-Roche. It is illegal in the United States and Canada, but in some countries in Europe and South America, it is used to treat insomnia and anxiety. It increases the high from other drugs and might make a person feel drunk. Rohypnol is ten times more potent than Valium, and its effects can be felt within fifteen minutes and may last for eight hours.[14] Although it has been considered the new "party" drug, Rohypnol can be very dangerous and even fatal in combination with alcohol or other drugs because it causes all of the body's functions to slow down significantly.[15] A month before his suicide in 1994, rock star Kurt Cobain had overdosed on a combination of Rohypnol and champagne.[16]

Rohypnol's most notable side effect, and the one that has sparked the most concern, is short-term amnesia. Users do not remember what happened while they were under the drug's influence. Because the drug is odorless and tasteless, victims often do not know they are even taking the drug. It may be slipped into a drink unnoticed.

Because of this, Hoffman-La Roche has changed the formulation of the drug so that it dissolves more slowly and releases a blue color in liquids. So that it can be more easily seen, parts of the tablet will also float in a dark drink such as cola.[17] There are many old tablets left, however, so people still need to be cautious. People should always know exactly what is in their beverages. Partygoers should get their own drinks or accept drinks only from those people they know and trust.

Though tranquilizing drugs can be used positively and can be very helpful, the negative aspects of their abuse often overshadow their intended benefits.

Unfortunately, tranquilizers (and other drugs) can be slipped into dark-colored drinks unnoticed. People should always be careful and be aware of exactly what is in any beverage that they drink.

three

Who Is Using and Abusing Downer Drugs?

Some people do use tranquilizer drugs responsibly. For these people, depressants are helpful and sometimes even necessary. Unfortunately, many people, both young and old, have problems with downer drugs. Sometimes even rich and famous people become abusers—money and fame do not keep a person away from the dangers of drugs. Stories about these celebrities sometimes have happy endings, but just like people who are not famous, sometimes their lives also end in tragedy.

Judy Garland was a person who lost her life to drugs, even though she became aware of the dangers of her drug use. She had tried to stop taking the drugs many times. She had had some frightening experiences with the drugs, including a couple of close calls during overdoses. She was always afraid that she would suffer the same fate as

Marilyn Monroe, who died in 1962, probably from accidentally taking too many barbiturates.

In his book *Rainbow: The Stormy Life of Judy Garland*, author Christopher Finch wrote,

> Judy supposed that Marilyn had taken pills to go to sleep, that they had had only a temporary effect, and when she woke—or half-woke—she took another batch of pills, forgetting how many she had already taken. The cumulative impact of these doses had been enough to kill her.[1]

When doctors examined Marilyn Monroe's body after she died of an apparent drug overdose, they did not find any evidence of the cause of her death. But Judy Garland continued to fear such an end for herself, and perhaps this it is what happened when she died on June 21, 1969. Because of the human body's ability to build up a tolerance to a drug, regardless of the amount that may cause an overdose, this situation was something Judy Garland worried about. Still, her death was a shock to her family and her fans. She was only forty-seven, and she left three children and millions of admirers behind to mourn her.

Some Famous Battles With Downer Drugs

Other stories do not end as sadly as Garland's. Some people have worked hard to overcome their addictions. One such story is that of Matthew Perry, one of the stars of the television show *Friends*. In 1997, Perry checked himself into a rehabilitation center in order to help overcome an addiction to the painkiller Vicodin™. Perry did not realize how easy it was to become addicted to the painkiller he started taking after his wisdom teeth were removed and then again after he was in an accident while jet skiing. The medication had been given to him by a doctor, but it was not difficult for his body to become dependent on it. At the time, his publicist said that he was in "the early stages of chemical dependency," and Perry was proud that he was able to stop using the painkiller before his problems got worse.[2] He told *TV Guide*, "Anything can come at me now, and I feel like I can take it because I got myself through that."[3]

NFL football player Brett Favre had similar feelings in 1997 about his triumph over the same drug, Vicodin. He started taking the drug to help him recover from injuries he received while playing quarterback for the Green Bay Packers and to help him handle the stress of the fame brought on by being named the NFL's Most Valuable

Brett Favre, who is the quarterback of the Green Bay Packers in the National Football League overcame an addiction to the downer drugs known as painkillers.

Player three times. He became dependent on the drug both physically and psychologically. His body needed the drug, and more significantly, he *thought* he needed it. The drug relaxed him and made him feel as if he could take on the world, though Favre said he never took the drug before or during a game.[4] He knew that he needed to stop taking the drug, though, because it affected the way he acted and made him sick. He suffered a serious seizure, which he initially thought was caused by a withdrawal from Vicodin. After his seizure, Favre realized he needed help, and thankfully, he was able to get it and move on with his life, free of drugs. He stopped taking the pills and later entered a rehabilitation center. With the help of his family and friends, Favre overcame his addiction. In his autobiography, Favre said,

> Now, I'd be lying if I said quitting was easy. . . . [S]lowly, I started to get my priorities straight again. Everyday, I would think about Deanna and Brittany [his wife and daughter] and our future together. I would think about all that I wanted to accomplish in football.[5]

The famous singer and movie star Elvis Presley, on the other hand, never realized that he was abusing drugs. He did not think it was a problem to use prescription medications. He strongly opposed the use of illegal drugs and was angry when he heard about anyone he knew taking "street drugs," as he called them.[6] In 1977, Presley's dependence on prescription medications was fatal. His body could not handle the buildup of so many years of drug abuse.

The rock star Jimi Hendrix also died as a result of downer drug use. One night in 1970 he took some barbiturates to help him sleep, and because the drugs slowed his breathing and the reflexes in his throat,

Elvis Presley never realized that he was abusing the prescription medications he was taking. Unfortunately, his body could not handle the buildup of so many years of drug abuse, and his dependence on these medicines was fatal.

Hendrix died from his overdose when he choked on his own vomit.[7]

Some famous people have overcome their drug problems and gone on to help other people do the same. Former first lady Betty Ford made headline news when she told the world about her addictions to alcohol and tranquilizers. She was one of the first people to show the public that addicts can overcome their addiction and that asking for help is not shameful. Many people have been helped because Betty Ford showed them that it is drug abuse, not the drug abuser, that is "bad."

Young People and Downer Drugs

Young people are just as vulnerable to drugs as adults. Because their bodies are still developing, however, prescription use of depressants in young people must be monitored closely and abuse must be stopped before a tragedy occurs. Using tranquilizers or sedative-hypnotics in a hospital setting or by prescription from a doctor is not something to be afraid of, but doctors must make sure their patients understand the dangers of abuse and the risk of tolerance and dependence.

Sometimes, tolerance and dependence are inevitable. This was the case with an eight-year-old boy whose legs were seriously injured in a lawn mower accident. He needed surgery but was in severe pain afterward. He was given morphine, a painkiller, while his wounds healed. He had to use the drug for several weeks. During this time, his body became dependent on the drug. The doctors closely watched the boy's dependence, and when it came time to take him off the drug, the hospital slowly reduced the doses he was receiving so that he did not suffer from any withdrawal

Former first lady Betty Ford made headlines when she admitted her addictions to alcohol and tranquilizers.

symptoms.[8] The boy had become dependent, but because he was properly cared for, he did not start to abuse his medication. He was not an addict.

Sometimes young people are prescribed tranquilizers for anxiety, nervousness, and aggression. Doctors do not usually like to prescribe long-term medications to children unless it is absolutely necessary. The drugs can sometimes affect growth and development. Also, doctors do not want young people growing up thinking that they need a drug if they do not. Drug abuse or misuse can cause serious problems in a young person's physical and mental development.

Unfortunately, many young people do abuse downer drugs. Some first begin using downers under a doctor's care. Others try them, illegally, with friends. Sometimes young people are even given drugs by family members who try to help them get through a tough time, such as the death of a loved one. This is what happened with one young man who abused heroin, a dangerous opioid that is often injected intravenously. He told doctors,

> I was three months away from my twelfth birthday. I went home for my mom's funeral and I saw my step-dad fixing [injecting heroin]. I asked him what it was for, he said to make himself feel better. . . . I asked him if it would make me feel better about mom dying and he said it would. He got into the habit of fixing me at least once a day.[9]

The boy abused heroin, but an adult was helping him do it. Both he and his stepfather had a serious problem, and both needed medical and psychological counseling to end their addictions.

Signs and Symptoms of Abuse

It is often difficult to tell when a person is abusing downer drugs. These drugs have an effect on every part of the body, however, and there *are* some visible signs and symptoms of abuse that can be recognized. A drug-abusing person may have a drooping head and eyelids, a slowed walk, and slowed or slurred speech. The pupils of the eyes may look like pinpoints if someone is using opioids, though there is not a big change in pupil size for a person who is using barbiturates. An opioid user may also suffer from very dry skin, constipation, and a changed hormonal system.[10] An abuser of depressant drugs may be overly calm but, depending on the situation, may also become anxious and even hostile. There are also some mental disorders associated with the use of depressants. Downer drug use may cause amnesia (loss of memory), severe anxiety, delirium (a state of extreme excitement), drastic mood shifts, sexual disorders, and sleeping problems.

But why do these things happen? Let us look at some of the physical and chemical effects of downer drugs and at the history of tranquilizing medications.

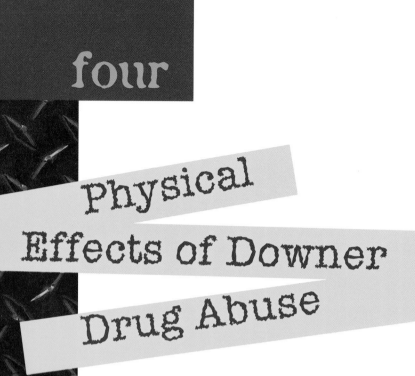

four

Physical Effects of Downer Drug Abuse

Downer drugs are nothing new. People have been using tranquilizing drugs throughout history. Opium, a drug that comes from the milklike liquid of the unripened opium poppy flower, has been an ingredient in tranquilizers for thousands of years. People in ancient times knew about the different effects of tranquilizers, and they knew these drugs could be helpful as well as deadly.

The History of Downer Drugs

Researchers have found evidence that people used opium even in prehistoric times. It was used as medicine in ancient Greece and Rome.[1] People in ancient Sumeria, Egypt, and China left records that show that they saw opium as a potential cure, a source of pleasure, and a poison.[2] The raw material of opium was used throughout the Middle

Ages, but because it had a bitter taste and the concentration of active ingredients was low, abuse of the drug was rare at this time.

When the tobacco pipe was brought from North America to Europe and Asia in the 1500s, people began to smoke opium and abuse started to spread.[3] When the hypodermic needle was invented in the mid-nineteenth century, people were able to get drugs into their bodies by a faster means than smoking. Abuse skyrocketed, but people did not fully recognize the dangers of drug use until later.

There have been serious worldwide conflicts about opium. There were wars between Great Britain and China in the 1800s, called the Opium Wars, when the two countries fought over the exclusive right to trade opium. There are still serious conflicts around the world between countries that produce drugs illegally and the countries where these drugs are bought and sold. Today there are other problems, because people can die if they

Opium, a drug that comes from the liquid found in the unripened poppy flower, has been an ingredient in tranquilizers for thousands of years. A field of opium poppy flowers is shown here.

contract AIDS by sharing the needles they use to inject downer drugs.

In the 1800s, scientists and doctors began to identify the different ingredients of the plants they were using to help their patients. In 1806, morphine was first processed from opium into tablets and injectable liquids, and it was thought to be a miracle drug. Doctors were incorrect when they thought it was not addictive. After the hypodermic needle was invented, morphine became easier to abuse for both patients and addicts. During the American Civil War, for example, morphine was used so often and so freely that a whole population of addicts resulted. Morphine addiction became known as the

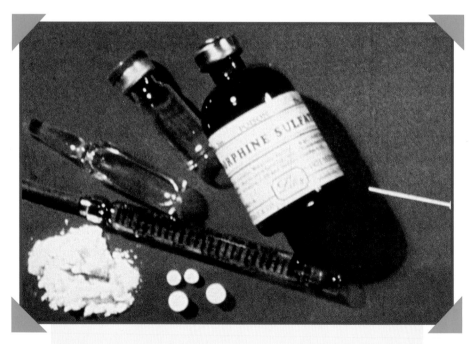

In 1806, morphine was first processed from opium into tablets and injectable liquids. It was originally thought to be a miracle drug—until doctors realized its potential for abuse.

"soldier's disease," and it was a very serious problem both during and after the war. Morphine can be very effective, however, for pain relief. Doctors today still measure pain by how much morphine it would take to relieve a patient's discomfort.

In the 1830s, codeine, another drug that comes from opium, was developed. Like morphine, it is still used today under closely controlled circumstances. Heroin was developed at the turn of the twentieth century when scientists tried to find an effective painkiller that was not likely to be abused or addictive. Heroin's effects, however, are intense and quick. Doctors and scientists were once again faced with a wonder drug that was not so wonderful after all.

Scientists continued to try to find a calming and painkilling drug that had no addictive or harmful side effects. They began to look into ingredients that did not include any opium products. The first step in this process was the discovery of barbituric acid in the 1860s. It was not until many years later, however, that its medicinal effects were understood. Barbital, the first barbiturate, was first used as medicine in 1882.[4] Once again, people soon realized that these new drugs had serious addictive qualities. They caused dependence and tolerance, and patients and nonpatients alike began to abuse them.

During the 1950s, benzodiazepines were created as scientists continued to try to find drugs with fewer side effects than opiates and barbiturates. Librium was the first benzodiazepine to be made, and it was first sold in 1960.

During the 1950s and 1960s, more people turned to drugs that affected both the body and mind. This type of drug is called a psychoactive drug. People thought that using these drugs was a safe and effective way of relieving anxiety and inducing sleep. The drugs were called "wonder drugs" or even "happiness pills" and "peace of mind drugs."[5] A drug called Miltown was even known as "mother's little helper" because it was often given to women who had young children. It was meant to help these women be less anxious when faced with the pressures of raising a family. The dangers of these drugs were realized only later.

Perhaps people would have acted differently if they had known how the drugs worked in the body and if they understood some of the major effects of downer drugs.

Downer Drugs and the Body

All psychoactive drugs change the way a person feels because of the way the drug gets to and enters the brain. The brain is a very complicated part of the body. It may be simpler to look at the brain in terms of the systems that help it to work. The limbic system, for example, is the area of the brain that causes feelings and emotions. It is in this area that depressant drugs primarily work.[6] Depressants also slow down activity in other places in the brain and in the spinal cord. They slow down other parts of the body that are not directly part of the central nervous system—the overall system that controls the body's physical responses as well as a person's behavior.

Drugs get into the brain through the blood and then by passing through the barrier separating the blood from the brain. If a drug crosses that barrier quickly, it will also leave quickly and will not remain in the brain for long. Drug abusers often want to use depressants that take effect quickly. These drugs, called "short" or "intermediate" acting depressants, can often be the most harmful because people continue taking them to prolong the effects.

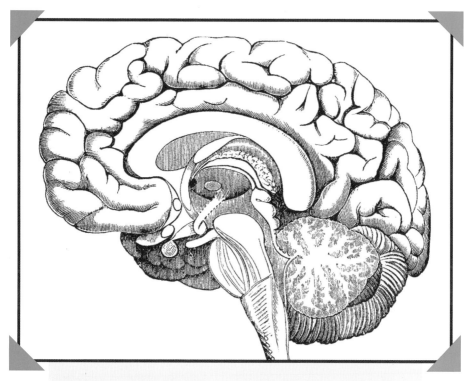

Downer drugs such as tranquilizers slow down the activity in the brain.

Dependence

Downer drugs can cause a person to become physically dependent if they are used for a long time. Being physically dependent means that a person's body needs the drug in order to function normally. It is as if the body gets so used to having the drug in the system that it becomes a routine part of the body's regular functions. Without the drug, a person may not be able to react normally and may feel worse than before the drug was taken. If a person is physically *and* psychologically dependent on a drug, a chain of abuse of one or more drugs might begin.

Psychological dependence is different from physical dependence, though a person may be dependent in both ways. When people are psychologically dependent on drugs, they *think* they need to take the drug in order to do everyday activities, and they may be afraid of what would happen if they were *not* taking the drug. People are therefore said to get addicted to feelings, not to the drugs themselves.[7] This is true in cases where people are psychologically dependent.

Physical dependence, on the other hand, affects how the body itself works and functions. Some people argue that both kinds of dependence are "enslaving," that drug users cannot escape from them. They say it is as if the drugs have control over their life as much, if not more, than the anxiety or depression did before they began using the drugs.

Barbara Gordon wrote about her experience with Valium dependence in the book *I'm Dancing as Fast as I Can*. She asked, "Why am I a slave to these pills?"[8] She was physically and psychologically dependent on medication prescribed to her by her doctor, and she needed help. As many dependent people discover, the dependence may cause more troubles than the original anxiety did.

Addiction is more than dependence. A person is addicted to a drug when he or she thinks only about getting the next dose of the drug. A drug addict will often go to great lengths to get more drugs.

In his book *Drug and Alcohol Abuse*, Dr. H. Thomas Milhorn reminds people that dependence is very serious, and he says that "Chemical dependence is an illness. . . . It is chronic; that is, it takes place over a period of time. . . . It is progressive; that is, it gets worse over time if it is not treated."[9] The most important thing to remember is that dependence is a disease and that a dependent person can get help to end a drug problem.

Tolerance

The drug's ability to cause tolerance in the body is one of the reasons a person may become dependent on a drug. Once the body becomes accustomed to a drug's presence in the bloodstream, a tolerance may build—in other words, a person's body may need more and more of the drug in order to feel the drug's effects. This can be very dangerous, especially when a drug user gets to the point where it takes a large amount of a drug to produce even small results.

For many downer drugs, as tolerance sets in, the amount needed for the effect gets higher, but the lethal dose stays the same. This means that though the amount of a drug necessary to produce the desired effects rapidly increases in the frequent user, the amount of the drug that will cause death remains the same. Some people think that this may be what happened to Judy Garland. She may have felt it necessary to take a higher dosage of the barbiturate Seconal in order to sleep that night. That dosage proved fatal, even though she may not have actually felt the drug's effects. Another important thing to know is that a tolerance to one kind of drug means that a person often is tolerant to other drugs that are similar. This is called cross-tolerance. A person with a tolerance to heroin, for example, will also be tolerant to drugs such as morphine. Tolerance can happen even if a person is following doctor's orders.

Withdrawal

People will know they are dependent on a drug if they have withdrawal symptoms when they stop taking the drug. Withdrawal symptoms are the body's way of showing the difficulties it has when it does not have the drug it has come to expect. Sometimes withdrawal symptoms are simply mild anxiety and insomnia, but sometimes they can be very severe. Depending on the drug and how long the person was using it, withdrawal symptoms may include irritability, panic attacks, depression, lack of energy, shakiness, headaches, nausea, or other flulike symptoms. If the withdrawal is very intense, a person may also suffer seizures, severe psychological reactions, and extreme exhaustion. Sometimes withdrawal can even be fatal especially with some depressant drugs such as Valium. More people have died withdrawing from Valium than from overdosing on it.[10]

Thankfully, the intensity of withdrawal may be lessened if a person stops taking the drug gradually. In order to do this, a person must slowly decrease the amount of the drug taken. This act of slowly diminishing the amount of the drug in a person's body is useful because it helps the body adjust more easily. This practice is used in hospitals and by doctors who are helping their patients quit both prescription medications and illegal drugs. People should talk to doctors before they stop taking a sedative or tranquilizer prescription. Doctors will be able to help them stop using the drug without too much discomfort.

Doctors have found a way to help people who are addicted to heroin by following the techniques of gradual withdrawal. Doctors take advantage of cross-tolerance

Withdrawal from downer drugs can be fatal if it is not properly supervised. People have died withdrawing from Valium™, for instance.

and gradual withdrawal to help people end their addiction to heroin. This serious and illegal downer drug has no medical use, but some people use it because of its dramatic calming effect. A person who is dependent on heroin also has a dependence on other sedatives due to cross-tolerance. Therefore, during withdrawal, the heroin user is given methadone, a less damaging opioid. The dosage of methadone is then slowly decreased until the person is no longer dependent. This way, people may end their addiction to heroin safely and begin to live better, healthier lives.

Overdose

One of the most serious problems associated with drug use is the possibility of overdose. Overdose is exactly what it sounds like—a dose of a drug that is more than the body can handle. During an overdose of a downer drug, the body's functions may slow down so much, and so quickly, that the person's heart may even stop beating. Overdose may lead to death unless the victim receives immediate medical attention.

People who have developed a tolerance for a drug are at a greater risk of overdosing because they may not realize that they are taking a lethal amount of the drug. Also, if a person uses more than one sedative drug at a time in combination with alcohol, another "downer," overdose is a serious risk. The depressants may have different effects when they are used at the same time. People who use illegal drugs bought on the streets face increased danger of overdose because street drugs have

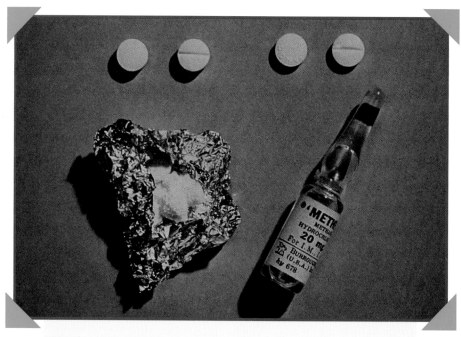

Heroin is a dangerous, illegal downer drug. A person who is dependent on heroin may be given methadone (shown here) during withdrawal.

unknown levels of purity or concentration. If a heroin user expects a dose of the drug to be 3 percent pure heroin, for example, but instead gets a dose with 30 percent pure heroin, the results could easily be fatal.[11]

Other Effects of Downer Drugs

While tranquilizers may show intense and immediate results, these drugs can have particularly serious long-term effects on the body. Barbiturates, for example, may cause a personality change. The user may suffer depression and irritability, drastic mood swings, or even odd and excited behavior.[12] There are many long-term risks involved with the use of prescription sleeping pills in particular, such as poor quality of sleep, daytime drowsiness, dependence, and insomnia (the inability to sleep) when the person stops taking the drug.[13]

Currently, barbiturates are thought to be very dangerous because they depress all of the body's functions—even a person's ability to breathe.[14] Benzodiazepines are thought to be safer than barbiturates for the average user because the amount of the drug needed to be effective is lower. However, there are still problems with benzodiazepines—they stay in the body's tissues for a long time, they are easily addictive, and there are serious dangers in the withdrawal process.

Addiction to both prescription and illegal drugs in the opium family is considered the deepest level of addiction possible, and these are often the hardest addictions to break. Heroin addiction is considered an epidemic that has affected many communities and threatens many more. Methaqualone, known on the streets as quaaludes, or simply "ludes," is a drug similar to barbiturates. Methaqualone was originally thought to be a good alternative to barbiturates because it was thought not to be addictive. It was used medicinally as a sleeping pill, but it was banned in the 1980s after widespread abuse. Addiction to quaaludes is a serious problem in many communities.

People need to be very careful to follow their doctors' instructions about the drugs they are prescribed. They should never take drugs that have not been prescribed or take drugs in ways other than as recommended by the prescription.

The Many Masks of Downer Drugs

Most drugs are known by many different names. Sometimes it is difficult to know which drug is which.

Downer Nicknames

Trade or Generic Names	Street Names
Codeine	loads, sets, 4s & doors
Heroin	dope, horse, smack, junk
Dolophine, Morphine	juice, God's medicine, Murphy, "M"
Laudanum, Pantopon	Dover's, Powder, O, op, tar
Barbiturates	barbs, beans, downers
Seconal	reds, red devils, seccies
Valium	vals
Librium, Libritabs	libs
Rohypnol	ruffies, rophies, roofies, roaches
Quaalude	ludes
Miltown	mother's little helper
Doriden	goofballs, goofers

There are names that scientists and doctors use, names that drug companies use, and names that addicts and abusers use. Sometimes a drug's nickname comes from the way the drug looks, or sometimes it comes from the way the drug's official name sounds. Nicknames may also be different, depending on what city the drugs are found in.

five

Fighting Abuse of Downer Drugs

There are certain groups of people who are at particular risk for abuse and misuse of drugs, especially tranquilizers or sedatives. Abuse of these drugs is a special problem for former addicts or those prone to alcoholism, for the elderly, and for women and children.

People at Risk—Alcoholics

People who have a problem with alcohol abuse are often more susceptible to the abuse of depressant drugs. This is because alcohol also acts as a depressant. Many downer drugs make people feel drunk. Therefore, people who are alcoholics may take downer drugs to make themselves drunk without using alcohol. In particular, studies have shown that people with a history of alcoholism tend to use more benzodiazepines than any other downer drugs.[1]

The Elderly

The elderly make up a significant portion of people using tranquilizers and sedatives. Unfortunately, there is quite a bit of misuse of depressant medication in this group of people. When older people are in nursing homes, they may find themselves at risk of overmedication. Studies show that nearly one in five elderly nursing home residents is exposed to potentially excessive use of tranquilizers. Nearly one fourth to one half receive some kind of tranquilizer or sedative routinely.[2] Many times, the elderly are given several different drugs at the same time, some of which should not be combined. Sometimes they remain on the drugs for longer than necessary at dosage

People who have problems with alcohol abuse are often more susceptible to the abuse of downer drugs such as tranquilizers.

levels that may be harmful. Doctors and patients need to monitor their drug use so it does not become a problem.

Women

While studies indicate that older people take more depressants than younger people, they also show that more women than men are likely to use prescription tranquilizers and sedatives. On the other hand, women are less likely than men to drink alcohol.[3] Why is there this difference between men and women? Women as a group are in better health than men and logically should not receive more prescriptions. Many doctors and sociologists have wondered about this phenomenon. One writer, Stephen Kandall, argues that many of the problems women have with depressant drugs started after World War II: "Women increasingly turned to psychoactive drugs. In some cases, prescription drugs were used to readapt women who had gained job satisfaction during the war to roles as housewives once again."[4] During the war, many women worked for the first time, and many felt very anxious when they gave up their jobs to soldiers returning from the war. It was at about this time that Miltown became a popular drug, and soon, it was commonly known as mother's little helper. The Rolling Stones even wrote a song about it.

The problem of women's drug use is also a serious concern because of the effects of drugs on newborns and infants. Pregnant women run the risk of seriously harming their unborn children if they use or abuse most drugs. If a woman thinks she is pregnant, she should consult her doctor for advice. When a pregnant woman uses drugs, her baby is also exposed to them. Babies born to abusers of heroin or barbiturates have been found to

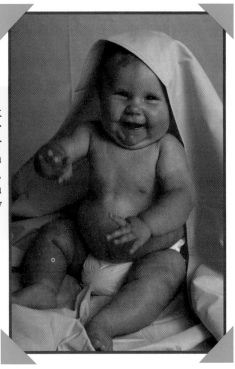

Pregnant women run the risk of seriously harming their unborn children if they use or abuse drugs. If a woman thinks she may be pregnant, she should consult with a doctor before taking any medications.

be hyperactive, to have difficulty sleeping and concentrating, and even to have tremors or the shakes.[5] Children born to women who have abused opiates such as heroin may also suffer from depression of the central nervous system. They may have severe convulsions a few days after birth because of withdrawal symptoms that occur when they are no longer exposed to the drug in the mother's womb. Women who abuse benzodiazepines such as Valium may give birth to children with muscle problems, severe sluggishness, breathing troubles, and facial deformities.[6] Drug-using mothers can also transfer opiates, benzodiazepines, and barbiturates to the baby through breast milk. Infants who are nursed by drug-using mothers may have withdrawal symptoms when either the drug-using or the breast-feeding stops.

Thalidomide

One sedative drug that seriously affected newborns in the past is Thalidomide. If a woman took Thalidomide while she was pregnant, her baby would often be born with a serious limb deformity—missing arms and legs resulted in hands attached at the shoulders and feet attached at the hips. A mother's use of Thalidomide may also have caused many other internal and external problems.

Thalidomide was developed in West Germany in the 1950s, but most countries had outlawed it by the early 1960s when the serious side effects became evident. Doctors learned that it did not matter how much Thalidomide a woman had taken, but *when* she had taken it. Some women had taken Thalidomide before they even knew they were pregnant. Thalidomide was never FDA-approved in the United States and legal only for a short time in Canada, where it was most often prescribed as a sedative.[7]

The question of Thalidomide resurfaced in the United States in the late 1990s. Scientists were surprised to discover that the drug was effective in clearing up the skin lesions caused by leprosy. Doctors decided to try to get the drug legitimized for treating leprosy and other ailments, including AIDS. Doctors succeeded in lifting the ban on Thalidomide in the United States, but there are strict regulations to prevent women from inadvertently taking the drug while pregnant.[8]

Prescription Regulations

There is now a system to prevent women from inadvertently harming their unborn children with Thalidomide. There are also regulations to control the prescription of other sedatives and tranquilizers. Doctors and lawmakers alike have realized that some patients will still try to get too much of a drug, either for their own use or to sell it to others. One California woman once tricked forty-two doctors and twenty-six pharmacies into giving her thousands of codeine tablets. Because of a glitch in the system of safety checks, her medical insurance even paid for the prescriptions. This kind of activity is illegal, and when the woman was caught, she was convicted and sent to jail.[9]

The Drug Enforcement Administration (DEA) estimates that several hundred million prescription drug doses are used for unnecessary and illegal reasons.[10] To help correct this problem, there are prescription monitoring programs in many states. In some of these programs, doctors are asked to write out multiple copies of prescriptions. The doctors write the prescription notes and give copies of the notes to an enforcement agency. The notes are lined up with other prescription notes to make sure that drugs are only used for useful medical reasons. Unfortunately, the computer systems used to control the regulation of prescription medications are often old. Because the information is usually slowly entered by hand, human error is always possible. All of the information may not end up in the system.

To help law enforcement agencies control illegal drug use, the United States government has divided drugs into different categories called schedules. The system was set up in 1970 when President Richard Nixon signed the Comprehensive Drug Abuse Prevention and Control Act. Schedule I drugs are those with a high potential for abuse and dependence and with no current acceptable medical uses. Schedule I drugs include heroin, LSD, marijuana,

Schedule Drugs

Schedule	Description	Examples
Schedule I	There is a high potential for abuse. There are no currently acceptable medical uses, and there is a lack of accepted safety for use, even under medical supervision.	heroin, LSD, marijuana, methaqualone
Schedule II	There is a high potential for abuse. There are currently acceptable medical uses (some with severe restrictions). Abuse may lead to severe psychological or physical dependence.	morphine, PCP, cocaine, methadone, methamphetamine
Schedule III	The potential for abuse is lower than that of Schedule I or II drugs, but risk is still present. There are currently accepted medical uses. Abuse may lead to moderate or low physical dependence or high psychological dependence.	anabolic steroids, Tylenol with codeine, some barbiturates
Schedule IV	There is low potential for abuse compared with the other schedules. There are currently accepted medical uses. Abuse may lead to limited physical or psychological dependence.	prescription tranquilizers
Schedule V	There is low potential for abuse compared with other schedules. There are currently accepted medical uses. Abuse may lead to physical or psychological dependence.	over-the-counter cough medicines with codeine

Source: DEA's Web site at <http://www.usdoj.gov/dea/pubs/abuse/chap1/contents.htm>.

and Rohypnol. At the other end of the list are Schedule V drugs, which have a very low potential for abuse and dependence as well as serving acceptable medical uses. Many of these latter drugs are available without prescription. The levels in between are for drugs that have acceptable medical uses but may have the potential for abuse and dependence. Many depressant drugs fall in between—they may have acceptable medical uses, but they may also be drugs that people abuse.

Fighting Abuse and Stopping It Before It Starts

How can doctors help their patients to not abuse their prescribed medications? The most important thing a doctor can do is make sure a patient is informed about all aspects of the prescribed medication and to make sure that the patient knows to ask questions about anything not understood. Doctors try to watch which medications a person is taking and make sure that the patient really needs the prescribed drugs.

Doctors, however, are not the only ones who need to know about the different aspects of drugs. Everyone should know what the effects of drugs are in order to make an informed decision about whether or not to take a drug. Many young people do not know about the various side effects if they take drugs illegally. They are at a very great risk of becoming drug abusers simply because they do not know that they are on a path toward abuse. It is important for people to realize that no drug is without some side effects and that no drug is perfect. Drugs affect a person's body in many ways. While sometimes these can be positive changes, sometimes they can also be very negative. When people use drugs without a doctor's prescription, they put themselves at a great risk of dependence, abuse, overdose, and even death.

How to Help

Young people can get involved in the fight against drug abuse first by becoming educated about drugs. It is necessary to understand something before you can fight it. After people know about the dangers, they can get involved in school or community programs that try to get the message out to other people.

Young people also need to realize that when they see actors using drugs in movies, they are probably seeing only one side of the issue—movies sometimes do not show the negative ways abuse can effect a person's body and mind. They often show only the high people get from the drugs, not the pain that comes afterward. By recognizing this and by helping other people see it as well, young people can do more than simply say "no" when they are offered drugs. Young people have to

Once young people learn about the dangers associated with downer drugs (and other drugs of abuse), they can get involved in school or community programs that try to get the message out to other people.

understand why they are saying "no" so they can feel more comfortable and confident about refusing drugs offered to them—even if they are being offered drugs by a friend. All drugs can be dangerous. By understanding all the ways a drug works and all the things that can happen when using drugs, young people can stop drug abuse.

Young people are sometimes drawn to drugs because they feel pressure from their friends to try them. A true friend will accept a decision to say no to drugs. When drug users try to get someone to try a drug, they may even make fun of the person for not trying it. The drug users often are simply trying to make themselves feel better about their own drug use. Peer pressure can be very powerful. Sometimes it is helpful to have an answer prepared beforehand, just in case drugs are ever offered. It is also helpful to look ahead to times when peer pressure might be an issue—and then to avoid those situations.

Getting Help

If people need help with drug abuse problems or if they think they are dependent on a drug, they should get help. They should talk to someone they trust. Quitting drugs will be a long process—and one they will have trouble doing alone. People have to choose to start drug treatment—if they are forced into it, the treatment is often ineffective.

One of the most important things when deciding to stop using downer drugs is to withdraw from them gradually. It is very helpful if a doctor or mental health professional is involved so that a person can withdraw successfully without harmful or painful withdrawal symptoms. Some people recommend that a schedule for withdrawal be written down so that a person can see the evidence of progress.[11]

Addiction and abuse are difficult things to overcome. It is much easier to be successful with the help and support of others. Many drug rehabilitation centers have therapy programs already set up, and a recovering addict may also want to join a group such as Alcoholics Anonymous (AA) or Narcotics Anonymous (NA). AA is a group that follows a twelve-step approach to ending addition, and there are many groups that use a similar model. In a twelve-step program, there is no therapist or doctor leading the group meeting. People in the group rely on other members for knowledge and support in order to stop drug or alcohol abuse. According to experts in the field of stopping drug abuse, "The twelve-stop process engages addicts at their level of addiction, breaks the isolation, guilt, and pain, and shows them they are not alone."[12]

The following page shows the twelve steps in the AA program. These steps are also used in groups that deal with other addiction problems.

There are also support groups such as Al-Anon to help people who are dealing with a loved one's drug or alcohol use. Groups like Alateen help young people cope with the problems that come from having an alcoholic as a family member or friend. It is a group specifically for young people because they may feel more comfortable talking with people their own age. Many twelve-step groups advertise in local phone books or newspapers, but doctors, hospitals, and drug treatment centers can also provide information about meeting times and places.

12-Step A A Program

1. We admitted we were powerless over alcohol [or other drugs, gambling, overeating, etc.]—that our lives had become unmanageable.

2. We came to believe that a Power greater than ourselves could restore us to sanity.

3. We made a decision to turn our will and our lives over to the care of God as we understand Him.

4. We made a searching and fearless moral inventory of ourselves.

5. We admitted to God, to ourselves, and to another human being the exact nature of our wrongs.

6. We were entirely ready to have God remove all these defects of character.

7. We humbly asked Him to remove our shortcomings.

8. We made a list of all persons we had harmed, and became willing to make amends to them all.

9. We made direct amends to such people wherever possible, except when to do so would injure them or others.

10. We continued to take personal inventory and when we were wrong promptly admitted it.

11. We sought through prayer and meditation to improve our conscious contact with God as we understood Him, praying only for knowledge of His will for us and the power to carry that out.

12. Having had a spiritual awakening as the result of these steps, we tried to carry this message to alcoholics [or drug abusers, gamblers, overeaters, etc.] and to practice these principles in all our affairs.[13]

People need to learn how to relieve anxiety and nervousness without using tranquilizers or sedative drugs. An anxious person should talk to a doctor about alternatives to drug use. Many people find that regular exercise, a balanced diet, and plenty of sleep may help calm them down. Drugs cannot substitute for the skills people have to relieve anxiety or even to have a good time. If people are involved with activities and take the time to talk to others, they will be able to resist drugs more easily.

questions
for discussion

1. What are some of the reasons that people give when asked why they began to use downer drugs? Why do some people begin to abuse downer drugs?

2. Why are downer drugs dangerous?

3. Why are downer drugs sometimes helpful and necessary?

4. What are dependence and tolerance?

5. Why does tolerance cause a serious risk for downer drug users?

6. Why is it dangerous to just stop taking downer drugs if a person has been taking them for a long time?

7. What are some things people can do to make themselves calm or happy without using drugs?

8. Why do you think groups that follow the twelve-step model are effective?

9. What is something a person could say if offered drugs by a friend?

chapter notes

Chapter 1. A Rainbow's End

1. James Spada with Karen Swenson, *Judy and Liza* (Garden City, N.Y.: Doubleday & Co., Inc., 1983), p. 17.

2. Christopher Finch, *Rainbow: The Stormy Life of Judy Garland* (New York: Grosset & Dunlap Publishers, Inc., 1975), p. 73.

Chapter 2. Social Effects of Downer Drugs

1. "High Anxiety," *Consumer Reports*, January 1993, p. 23.

2. Phillip W. Long, M.D., "Generalized Anxiety Disorder," © 1995–1997, <http://www.mentalhealth.com>, September 14, 1999.

3. Cynthia Kuhn, Scott Swartzwelder, and Wilkie Wilson, *Buzzed: The Straight Facts About the Most Used and Abused Drugs from Alcohol to Ecstasy* (New York: W.W. Norton & Company, Inc., 1998), p. 184.

4. John Cottingham, "The Parkinsn List Drug Database," December 12, 1998, <http://www.ionet.net/~jcott/homepage/drugdb/045.html>, September 14, 1999.

5. Ann Marie Pagliaro and Louis A. Pagliaro, *Substance Abuse Among Children and Adolescents* (New York: John Wiley & Sons, Inc., 1996), p. 7.

6. Dan Weikel, "Prescription Fraud: Abusing the System," *The Los Angeles Times*, August 18, 1996, p. A25.

7. Darryl S. Inaba, William E. Cohen, and Michael E. Holstein, *Uppers, Downers, All Arounders: Physical and Mental Effects of Psychoactive Drugs* (Ashland, Oreg.: CNS Publications, Inc., 1997), p. 144.

8. Ibid., p. 65.

9. H. Thomas Milhorn, Jr., *Drug and Alcohol Abuse: The Authoritative Guide for Parents, Teachers, and Counselors* (New York: Plenum Press, 1994), p. 261.

10. Pagliaro and Pagliaro, p. 175; "High Anxiety," p. 21.

11. Gerry Oster, Daniel M. Huse, Shelly F. Adams, Joseph Imbimbo, and Mason W. Russell, "Benzodiazepine Tranquilizers and the Risk of Accidental Injury," *American Journal of Public Health*, December 1980, pp. 1467–1470.

12. Berger, p. 40.

13. Inaba et al., p. 153; Joanne Ross, Shane Darke, and Wayne Hall, "Transitions Between Routes of Benzodiazepine Administration Among Heroin Users in Sydney," *Addiction*, June 1997, p. 697.

14. Richard H. Schwartz and Andrea B. Weaver, "Rohypnol, The Date Rape Drug," *Clinical Pediatrics*, vol. 37, May 1998, p. 321; Arthur Santan and Charles W. Hall, "Banned 'Date Rape' Drug Is Linked to Six Assaults in Area," *The Washington Post*, June 14, 1996, p. B5.

15. Schwartz and Weaver, p. 321; Mireya Navarro, "In South, Drug Abusers Turn to a Smuggled Sedative," *The New York Times*, December 9, 1995, p. A6.

16. Navarro, p. A6.

17. "Drug Linked to Assaults Is Reformulated," *The New York Times*, October 19, 1997, section 1, p. 20.

Chapter 3. Who Is Using and Abusing Downer Drugs?

1. Christopher Finch, *Rainbow: The Stormy Life of Judy Garland* (New York: Grosset & Dunlap Publishers, Inc., 1975), pp. 243–244.

2. "Mathew Perry Checks Into Rehab," *People*, June 4, 1997, <http://www.mrshowbiz.go.com/news/Todays-Stories/970604/6_4_97_1perry.html> March 14, 1999.

3. "Matthew Perry on Rehab," *People*, June 16, 1997, <http://www.mrshowbiz.go.com/news/Todays-Stories/980427/perry42798.html> March 14, 1999.

4. Brett Favre with Chris Havel, *Favre: For the Record* (New York: Doubleday, 1997), p. 20.

5. Kevin Volkan, *Dancing Among the Maenads: The Psychology of Compulsive Drug Use* (New York: Peter Lang, 1994), p. 98.

6. Marilyn Carroll and Gary Gallo, *Quaaludes: The Quest for Oblivion* (New York: Chelsea House Publishers, 1995), p. 74; Volkan, p. 94.

7. Myron Yaster, Sabine Kost-Byerly, Charles Berde, and Carol Billet, "The Management of Opioid and Benzodiazapine Dependence in Infants, Children, and Adolescents," *Pediatrics*, vol. 98, no. 1, July 1996, p. 135.

8. Ann Marie Pagliaro and Louis A. Pagliaro, *Substance Abuse Among Children and Adolescents* (New York: John Wiley & Sons, Inc., 1996), pp. 134–135.

9. Darryl S. Inaba, William E. Cohen, and Michael E. Holstein, *Uppers, Downers, All Arounders: Physical and Mental Effects of Psychoactive Drugs* (Ashland, Oreg.: CNS Publications, Inc., 1997), p. 148.

10. Ibid.

Chapter 4. Physical Effects of Drug Abuse

1. Jonathan Gabe, *Understanding Tranquilizer Use: The Role of the Social Sciences* (New York: Routledge, 1991), p. 2.

2. Darryl S. Inaba, William E. Cohen, and Michael E. Holstein, *Uppers, Downers, All Arounders: Physical and Mental Effects of Psychoactive Drugs* (Ashland, Oreg.: CNS Publications, Inc., 1997), p. 142.

3. Ibid., pp. 142–143.

4. H. Thomas Milhorn, Jr., *Drug and Alcohol Abuse: The Authoritative Guide for Parents, Teachers, and Counselors* (New York: Plenum Press, 1994), p. 258.

5. Stephen R. Kandall, *Substance and Shadow: Women and Addiction in the United States* (Cambridge, Mass.: Harvard University Press, 1996), p. 138.

6. Milhorn, p. 21.

7. Ibid.

8. Barbara Gordon, *I'm Dancing as Fast as I Can* (New York: Bantam Books, 1979), p. 43.

9. Milhorn, p. 106.

10. Inaba et al., p. 166.

11. Ibid., p. 153.

12. Ibid., p. 163.

13. Sally Squires, "Sleep Aids Are Popular, But Do They Work? Study Questions Effectiveness and Safety of Over-the-Counter Medicines," *Washington Post Health*, March 7, 1995, p. 7.

14. Cynthia Kuhn, Scott Swartzwelder, and Wilkie Wilson, *Buzzed: The Straight Facts About the Most Used and Abused Drugs from Alcohol to Ecstasy* (New York: W.W. Norton & Company, Inc., 1998), p. 183.

Chapter 5. Fighting Abuse of Downer Drugs

1. Lorne B. Warnecke, "Benzodiazepines: Abuse and New Use," *Canadian Journal of Psychiatry*, vol. 36, no. 3, April 1991, p. 196; Herminio Martinez-Cano, Antonio Vela-Bueno, Mariano De Iceta, Rolando Pomalina, Isabel Martinez-Graz, and Maria Paz Sobrino, "Benzodiazepine Types in High Versus Therapeutic Dose Dependence," *Addiction*, vol. 91, no. 8, August 1996, p. 1179.

2. Bonnie L. Svarstad and Jeanine K. Mount, "Nursing Home Resources and Tranquilizer Use Among the Institutional Elderly," *Journal of the American Geriatric Society*, vol. 39, no. 9, September 1999, pp. 873, 869.

3. Kathryn Graham and David Vidal-Zeballos, "Analyses of Use of Tranquilizers and Sleeping Pills Across Five Surveys of the Same Population: The Relationship With Gender, Age, and Use of Other Substances," *Social Science & Medicine*, vol. 46, no. 3, 1998, p. 392.

4. Stephen R. Kandall, *Substance and Shadow: Women and Addiction in the United States* (Cambridge, Mass.: Harvard University Press, 1996), p. 140.

5. "Children of Drug Addicts," *Encyclopedia of World Problems and Human Potential*, © 1999, <http://www.uia.org/uiademo/pro/e4609.htm>, September 14, 1999.

6. Ann Marie Pagliaro and Louis A. Pagliaro, *Substance Abuse Among Children and Adolescents* (New York: John Wiley & Sons, Inc., 1996), p. 7; H. Thomas Milhorn, Jr., *Drug and Alcohol Abuse: The Authoritative Guide for Parents, Teachers, and Counselors* (New York: Plenum Press, 1994), pp. 154–155.

7. Ethel Roskies, *Abnormality and Normality: The Mothering of Thalidomide Children* (Ithaca, N.Y.: Cornell University Press, 1972), p. 4.

8. Sheryl Gay Stolberg, "Thalidomide Approved to Treat Leprosy, With Other Uses Seen," *The New York Times*, July 17, 1998, pp. A1, A12.

9. Dan Weikel, "Prescription Fraud: Abusing the System," *The Los Angeles Times*, August 18, 1996, p. A24.

10. Report to the Chairman, Health Subcommittee, Ways and Means Committee, House of Representatives, "Prescription Drug Monitoring: States Can Readily Identify Illegal Sales and Use of Controlled Substances," July 1992, p. 1.

11. Heather Ashton, "The Treatment of Benzodiazepine Dependence," *Addiction*, vol. 89, no. 11, November 1994, p. 1536.

12. Darryl S. Inaba, William E. Cohen, and Michael E. Holstein, *Uppers, Downers, All Arounders: Physical and Mental Effects of Psychoactive Drugs* (Ashland, Oreg.: CNS Publications, Inc., 1997), p. 389.

13. Alcoholics Anonymous Home Page, © 1998, <http://www.aa.org/> March 14, 1999.

further reading

Buckalew, M. Walter. *Drugs and Stress*. New York: The Rosen Publishing Group, Inc., 1997

Clayton, Lawrence. *Tranquilizers*. Springfield, N.J.: Enslow Publishers, Inc., 1997.

———. *Barbiturates and Other Depressants*. New York: The Rosen Publishing Group, Inc., 1997.

Henningfield, Jack E., and Nancy Ator. *Barbiturates: Sleeping Potions or Intoxicants?* New York: Chelsea House Publishers, 1992.

Inaba, Darryl S. (Pharm. D.), William E. Cohen, and Michael E. Holstein, Ph.D. *Uppers, Downers, All Arounders: Physical and Mental Effects of Psychoactive Drugs*. 3rd edition. Ashland, Oreg.: CNS Publications, Inc., 1997.

Kuhn, Cynthia, Scott Swartzwelder, and Wilkie Wilson. *Buzzed: The Straight Facts About the Most Used and Abused Drugs from Alcohol to Ecstasy*. New York: W. W. Norton & Company, Inc., 1998.

Milhorn, Thomas H., Jr., M.D., Ph.D. *Drug and Alcohol Abuse: The Authoritative Guide for Parents, Teachers, and Counselors*. New York: Plenum Press, 1994.

internet addresses

Alcoholics Anonymous
<http://www.aa.org>

Drug Enforcement Administration
<http://www.usdoj.gov/dea>

Get It Straight! (a guide for kids from the DEA)
<http://www.usdoj.gov/dea/pubs/straight/toc.htm>

National Clearinghouse for Alcohol and Drug Information:
<http://www.health.org/index.htm>

National Institute on Drug Abuse
<http://www.nida.nih.gov>

Partnership for a Drug-Free America
<http://www.drugfreeamerica.org>

index